READY, SET, CODE!

The Unofficial Guide to **CODING** with **Minecraft**

Álvaro Scrivano
Illustrated by Sue Downing

Lerner Publications ◆ Minneapolis

MINECRAFT is a registered trademark of Mojang Synergies AB Corporation,
Stockholm, Sweden, and is used solely to identify the games which are the subject of
this book. MakeCode is a registered trademark of Microsoft Corporation. This book is a publication of
Lerner Publishing Group, Inc., Minneapolis,
Minnesota, and is not licensed, approved, sponsored or endorsed by Mojang
Synergies AB Corporation or Microsoft Corporation.

First American edition published in 2019 by Lerner Publishing Group, Inc.

First published in Great Britain in 2018 by Wayland
Copyright © Hodder and Stoughton, 2018
All rights reserved.

Editor: Hayley Fairhead
Design and illustrations: Collaborate

All rights reserved. International copyright secured. No part of this book may be reproduced, stored in
a retrieval system, or transmitted in any form or by any means—electronic, mechanical, photocopying,
recording, or otherwise—without the prior written permission of Lerner Publishing Group, Inc., except for
the inclusion of brief quotations in an acknowledged review.

Lerner Publications Company
A division of Lerner Publishing Group, Inc.
241 First Avenue North
Minneapolis, MN 55401 USA

For reading levels and more information, look up
this title at www.lernerbooks.com.

Main body text set in Frutiger LT Pro 45 Light.
Typeface provided by Linotype AG.

Library of Congress Cataloging-in-Publication Data

The Cataloging-in-Publication Data for *The Unofficial Guide to Coding with Minecraft* is on file at the
Library of Congress.
ISBN 978-1-5415-3877-1 (lib. bdg.)
ISBN 978-1-5415-4666-0 (pbk.)
ISBN 978-1-5415-4302-7 (eb pdf)

Printed in China
1-45060-35887-7/25/2018

Contents

What Is *Minecraft*?

Minecraft is a game where players can work with blocks to create wonderful, imaginative worlds. The game is used to teach lots of different subjects, from chemistry and coding to literature and mathematics.

Note to parents:

What you need to work on the projects in this book:

1. A Windows 10 device with a full version of *Minecraft* for Windows 10 installed upon it
2. Internet access

Online safety

- It is important that you read *Minecraft* game reviews to understand more about potential risks or difficulties.

- Talk to your child about what they are up to online and keep up-to-date with your child's development online.

- Set boundaries in the online world just as you would in the real world.

- Keep all equipment that connects to the internet in a family space. Do not let your child search the internet without supervision.

- Do not let your child play with others they do not know.

Installation

1. *Minecraft*

To code in *Minecraft*, you will need a full version (not just the X-Box version) of *Minecraft* installed on your desktop computer. *Minecraft* for Windows 10 can be accessed through the Windows app store. This is free for existing owners of the original *Minecraft* PC Java version, or you can buy it in the Windows app store. If you already own *Minecraft* for Windows 10, you need to ensure that you have the latest update.

2. Code Connection

Once you have the game installed, you need to install the Code Connection app, which you can download from **education. minecraft.net/get-started/download**. Once you install it, run it, and it should leave a shortcut on your desktop.

Now you have the full version of *Minecraft* and Code Connection, you can use Microsoft MakeCode to code your own *Minecraft* projects.

You will notice that for all the projects in this book, it is necessary to activate cheats in settings. "Cheating" is used to customize the running of the game by connecting with Code Connection.

MakeCode

When you open a new project in MakeCode, you will see the window below:

The toolbox is made of different menus.

Click here to see commands sent to *Minecraft*.

Click here to stop running MakeCode.

Click the snail icon to slow down your program.

You can go back and forth between Blocks and JavaScript editors.

Name your project and save it in your device.

Workspace
The project will be built here. Right-click to delete all blocks, format code, or download a screenshot of your program.

Make your blocks bigger or smaller by clicking on these signs.

Redo or undo the last step.

Deleting a block

There are three ways to delete a block in MakeCode:

A. Select the block and press the Delete button on the keyboard
B. Right-click on the block and select delete
C. Drag and drop the block into the toolbox

Controls in *Minecraft*

The mouse controls turning and aiming.

Left mouse button

The left button is used to hit things, either to break blocks or attack an enemy. It will use the item you are using in your main hand to hit things.

Right mouse button

The right button is used for a lot of things:

- using certain tools (hoeing farmland, shearing sheep)
- placing blocks
- firing bows (hold to build power, then release)
- throwing missiles (eggs, snowballs, splash potions)
- eating and drinking
- using the item in your off hand
- operating buttons and levers
- opening doors
- accessing containers (chests, furnaces, brewing stands, etc)

Button	Action
W	Forward (double-tap to sprint)
S	Backward
A	Left
D	Right
Space	Jump
Shift	Sneak

Tip
In Creative Mode, double-click the Space key to fly. When flying, press Space to move upward and Shift to move downward.

SUNFLOWER FIELD

DESIGN YOUR OWN SUNFLOWER FIELD!

READY »

Let's get started with *Minecraft*!

1

GETTING STARTED
Open *Minecraft* and click on Play.

2

CREATE A NEW WORLD
Click on Create New.

Click on Create New World in the next two stages.

③ CHOOSE THE GAME SETTINGS

Under Game Settings, choose the following options from each drop-down list:

Default Game Mode: Creative

Difficulty: Easy

World Type: Flat

Cheats: Activate Cheats should be on, with the toggle to the right.

Now click on the Create button on the left-hand side of the screen.

SET

You are now in *Minecraft*. Don't start playing yet! You need to code first!

④ PAUSE
Click Esc on your keyboard to pause the game.

Did you know?
Sunflowers can vary from 3 feet to a whopping 17.7 feet in height. They are one of the fastest growing plants, able to reach 8 to 12 feet in just 6 months.

5 OPEN CODE CONNECTION

Now go to your desktop and open Code Connection by double-clicking on the icon. You need to copy the command in the box by clicking on the double page icon on the right.

6 GO BACK TO *MINECRAFT*

Open *Minecraft* again and click on Resume Game

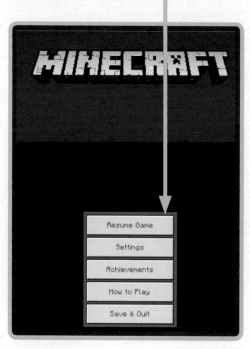

Tip

If a block you drop in the workspace is grayed out, it means it is disabled. You need to ensure you drop it inside a command or function block to enable it.

Now click on the letter T on your keyboard to open the chat box.

Paste (Ctrl+V) the link you copied from Code Connection in the dark gray box at the bottom and press Enter on your keyboard. A message should appear saying "Connection established to server."

Did you know?

There are around 60 different species of sunflower that are all native to North America.

7 LOAD MAKECODE

Go back to Code Connection and click on MakeCode. Microsoft MakeCode will load and then open.

8 START A NEW PROJECT

In MakeCode, go to My Projects and click on the plus sign.

CODE! »

Now you have everything you need to create your sunflower field animation.

9 SELECT A COMMAND BLOCK

Use the on chat command already on the workspace and type in the command "SF" followed by Enter on your keyboard. This block will run the code when you type the "SF" command in the game chat.

10 CHOOSE YOUR SUNFLOWER

From the BLOCKS menu, drag the fill with block and place it inside the on chat command block.

Click on the fill with drop-down menu and choose the sunflower.

Tip
If you cannot find the sunflower, type in "Sunflower" in the search box and it will appear.

11 SET PARAMETERS

You might have noticed that the fill with block has numbers below the sunflower. These numbers are called parameters in *Minecraft*. They mark the first corner of the area you are going to cover (from) to the opposite corner (to). Add the following parameters:

12 SET TIME AND WEATHER

You can choose the weather and the time for your animation. Choose the following two blocks from the GAMEPLAY menu and drop them below the fill with block. Your code should look like this:

Click on the drop-down menu and choose keep, as it will plant the sunflower on top of the existing blocks.

These blocks will set the time to midday and the weather to clear.

13 WRITE IN *MINECRAFT*

To add some text to the animation, go to BLOCKS and drag and drop the print block. Delete "Hello" and type in "This is my sunflower field," followed by Enter.

Where it says "of," click on the drop-down menu and choose Granite.

Finally, where it says "at," type in the parameters 0, 4, 0. Your code should look like this:

14

TEST YOUR ANIMATION

Open *Minecraft* and click T on your keyboard to open the chat box. In the chat box, type in the command "SF" and press Enter on your keyboard. Now click on Exit at the top of the screen. Move around to see the sunflower field and the text.

Did you know?

Kansas is often known as the Sunflower State, and the sunflower is Kansas's state flower. The sunflower is also the national flower of Ukraine.

CHALLENGE

Use your new skills and create a flower garden next to the sunflower field. Change the weather to rain.

TROUBLESHOOTING

When you run a code in *Minecraft*, your program will stay there. If you want to run your program again, delete your old creation by mining it (destroy what is in front of the agent by left-clicking on the mouse) or walk away from it and then run your program again in a different place.

SHEEP PEN
DESIGN A HOME FOR SOME SHEEP!

READY

Get *Minecraft* open, but don't start playing!

1 **GETTING STARTED**
Follow Steps 1 to 3 on pages 6 and 7 to open *Minecraft*.

SET

You are in *Minecraft*. Now you need to get everything ready to code!

2 **OPEN CODE CONNECTION AND MAKECODE**
Follow Steps 4 to 8 on pages 7 to 9 to open Code Connection and MakeCode.

CODE!

Now you can start creating your sheep pen.

3 **SELECT A COMMAND BLOCK**
Use the on chat command already on the workspace and type in the command "pen" and then press Enter. This block will run the code when you type the command in the game chat. Type in a command that will help identify your creation, such as "pen".

4 **ADD A FENCE**
From the BLOCKS menu, drag the place at block and drop it inside the on chat command block.

Click on the place drop-down menu and type in "Fence" in the search box. All the available fences will appear. Choose the one you like most for your animation.

Did you know?
The bighorn sheep is a species of sheep native to North America. It was named after its large, curled horns.

5

DUPLICATE A BLOCK
Right-click on the place at block and select Duplicate from the drop-down menu.

Repeat this until you have four place at blocks. Position all of these within the on chat command block.

6

POSITION THE FENCE
Type in the following parameters for your fences:

7

TURN THE AGENT
Go to the AGENT menu and drag the agent turn left block onto the workspace. Drop it inside on chat command under the last place at block.

8

COMPLETE THE FENCE
Add the other sides of the pen by repeating Steps 5–7. Then add the parameters as follows:

14

9 TEST YOUR PROGRAM

Go to *Minecraft* and click T on your keyboard to open the chat box. Type in "pen" and press Enter. Now click on Exit at the top of the screen. Do not forget to move around to look at your square pen. Try to fly up and see how it looks.

10 ADD THE SHEEP

For this part, you need to go inside the pen in *Minecraft*. Once you are there, press Esc to pause the game and return to MakeCode. You are going to add another command block for the sheep. Drag and drop a new on command chat from the PLAYER menu next to the pen program and type in "sheep".

11 USE LOOPS

For this part, you need to go to LOOPS and drag and drop the repeat block inside the on command chat block.

Did you know?
Sheep are social animals, and they love to stay in herds. A group of sheep is called a flock or mob.

12 ANIMAL SPAWNING

Go to the MOBS menu and drag the spawn animal at block inside the repeat block. Click on the drop-down menu and choose Sheep.

Drag your mouse over the picture and the name of the animal will appear.

Your program should look like this when it is finished in MakeCode:

13 TEST YOUR PROGRAM

Go to *Minecraft* and make sure you are inside the pen. Click T on your keyboard to open the chat box. Type in "sheep" and press Enter. Four sheep should be spawned inside the pen. Do not forget to move around to look at the sheep inside the pen. You program should look like this when it is finished in *Minecraft*:

CHALLENGE

Use your new skills and spawn more animals. Add a hungry wolf outside the pen looking at the sheep! Try to change the weather.

TROUBLESHOOTING

If the sheep are not inside the pen, it is because you have not moved inside the pen first. To solve this, while you are in *Minecraft* and before running the command "sheep", use your keyboard to move inside the pen (see page 5 for controls in *Minecraft*) and then run the sheep command.

If you think that there are too many sheep inside the pen, you need to change the number of animals spawned in the repeat block in the "sheep" command. Try a smaller number.

Did you know?

Sheep are able to see things to the front, side, and almost behind them without turning their heads because of the shape of their eyes.

RABBITS IN THE FOREST

CREATE A FOREST WITH RABBITS HOPPING AROUND!

READY >>

Get *Minecraft* open, but don't start playing!

1 GETTING STARTED
Follow Steps 1 to 3 on pages 6 and 7 to open *Minecraft*.

Did you know?
Rabbits can have as many as 25 babies in one year.

SET >>

Before you start coding, you need to open up MakeCode.

2 OPEN CODE CONNECTION AND MAKECODE
Follow Steps 4 to 8 on pages 7 to 9 to open Code Connection and MakeCode.

CODE! ➤➤

Now you're ready to create your rabbit animation!

3 **SELECT A COMMAND BLOCK**
Use the on chat command already on the workspace and type in the command "pond" followed by Enter. This block will run the code when you type the command in the game chat.

From the BLOCKS menu, drag the replace with block and drop it inside the on chat command block.

4 **CHOOSE BLOCKS**
Click on the drop-down menu in the replace with section and choose Water.

If you cannot find it, type in "Water" in the search box. Add the following parameters:

These blocks will replace the grass blocks with water blocks within the parameters shown here.

Did you know?
A female rabbit is called a doe, and a male rabbit is called a buck.

5

TELEPORT A PLAYER

After finishing the pond, the player needs to move to another place to create other parts for this animation. You need to use a teleport to block to move your player to another position. This block has parameters because you need to indicate where you want your player to be.

Go to the PLAYER menu and add the teleport to block underneath the replace with block and adjust the parameters.

6 CREATE THE FOREST

Drag and drop a new on chat command block from the PLAYER menu and type in "woods". Inside the on chat command block add a fill with block from the BLOCKS menu and search for Dark Oak Sapling trees. Finally, add a teleport to block from the PLAYER menu to move the player away once the forest program is complete. Adjust the parameters as follows:

These parameters will place the woods by the pond.

Select keep to plant the trees on top of the grass.

This block will move the player away after finishing the woods.

7 SET THE TIME AND WEATHER

Go to the LOOPS menu and drag and drop the on start block onto the workspace. Go to the GAMEPLAY menu and drag and drop the time set block inside the on start block, then add the weather block. Select rain from the drop-down menu.

The blocks should look like this:

8 ADD ANIMALS TO YOUR ANIMATION

You will add rabbits to your animation using a different command block. Go to the PLAYER menu and drag and drop the on player walk command onto the workspace. Inside this block, add the spawn animal block from the MOBS menu and choose rabbit from the drop-down list.

Your program should look like this when it is finished:

Did you know?
Rabbits have ears which can grow to as long as 4 inches.

Leave the parameters at 0,0,0. The rabbits will be spawned in the same place where the player is.

9 TEST YOUR PROGRAM

Go to *Minecraft* and click T on your keyboard to open the chat box. Type in "pond" and press Enter. Then type in "woods" and press Enter. Now click on Exit. Walk around and then turn. Do you see rabbits behind you? That is because your program spawns a rabbit every time you walk.

CHALLENGE
Change the time to midday and the weather to clear. Change the on player walk block to the on player swim block and change the animal. Go back to *Minecraft*, swim in the pond, and see what happens!

TROUBLESHOOTING
If you think that the woods are far away from the pond, you may need to change the parameters in the teleport to block in the "pond" command. Try -2 instead of -8 for the parameter in the first box.

FARMING

SOW SOME SEEDS AND WATCH THEM GROW!

READY ▶

Get *Minecraft* open, but don't start playing!

 GETTING STARTED
Follow Steps 1 to 3 on pages 6 and 7 to open *Minecraft*.

SET ▶

You are in *Minecraft*. Now you need to get everything ready to code!

 OPEN CODE CONNECTION AND MAKECODE
Follow Steps 4 to 8 on pages 7 to 9 to open Code Connection and MakeCode.

3 FILL IN YOUR INVENTORY

For this project, you will need to provide some seeds for the agent to plant.

Go back to *Minecraft* and click E on your keyboard. The inventory window will open up.

A. Type in the word "seeds" in the dark gray box.

B. Choose any seeds you like by clicking on them and dropping them in one of the slots at the bottom of the page.

C. Then click on either of these two icons to fill in the agent's inventory (see Step 4).

Tip

If you want to see what the agent has in his inventory, right-click on the agent and you will see the inventory.

FAIRTRADE
INTERNATIONAL

Did you know?

Fair trade is when farmers are given a fair amount of money for the products they produce. It makes sure that farmers in the developing world have better working conditions.

4

DRAG AND DROP ITEMS FROM THE INVENTORY

Drag the seeds from the inventory by clicking on the seeds.

Drop the seeds in the top left slot by clicking in the slot. The agent will drop what is in this slot first.

The seeds are now ready to be sown!

Tip
Hover the mouse pointer over the seeds to see their names.

CODE!

Now your agent can start farming!

5 **SOW THE SEEDS**
Use the on chat command already on the workspace and type in the command "sow" followed by Enter. This block will run the code when you type the command in the game chat.

6 **GET YOUR AGENT MOVING**
Drag and drop the following blocks from the AGENT menu:

This block will make the agent till soil forward.

This block will make the agent plant the seeds from the active inventory slot every time it moves.

This block will make the agent move forward by one block.

7 **TEST YOUR PROGRAM**
Go to *Minecraft*, open the chat box by clicking T on the keyboard and type in "sow". You should see the agent planting the seeds you added to the inventory.

8 USE LOOPS

Go back to MakeCode, drag the agent blocks (orange) outside the on chat command block and delete the on chat command block. Go to the LOOPS menu and choose a repeat 4 times block. Drop all the agent blocks (orange) inside the repeat block. This loop will help you make the agent repeat the actions without using the same block several times. You might have noticed that the loop you have just created is grayed out. This is because is does not have a function or command yet. You will add a function in the next step.

9 CREATE A FUNCTION

You are going to create a function to till the soil and plant the seeds.

Click on the ADVANCED menu.

More menus will appear below. Click on FUNCTIONS.

Click on Make a Function and name it "sow". Now drop the repeat 4 times block and agent blocks inside the function block. Your function should look like this:

10

CREATE ANOTHER FUNCTION

Create another function to make the agent turn.

As you did in Step 9, go to FUNCTIONS and click on Make a Function. Name it "turn". Go to the AGENT menu and drag and drop the agent move forward and agent turn blocks inside the function twice. Your function should look like this:

Did you know?

Fruit farming began between 6000 and 3000 BCE. Figs were one of the first cultivated fruit crops.

11

CREATE A COMMAND

Go to the PLAYER menu. Drag and drop the on chat command block and name it "farm". Go to the AGENT menu and select the agent teleport to player block to bring the agent to the player when "farm" is typed. Using the functions you created, let's make the agent sow, turn, and sow again. Finally, teleport the player away from the tilled soil to look at the agent's work. This part of the program should look like this:

12

USE A TRIGGER MESSAGE

Once the player is teleported, let's change the weather to water the seeds. Go to the PLAYER menu and drag and drop the on player teleported block. Then go to the GAMEPLAY menu and drag the weather block and select rain from the drop-down menu.

Your complete program should look like this when it is finished:

13

TEST YOUR PROGRAM
Go to *Minecraft* and press T on your keyboard to open the chat box. Type in "farm" and press Enter. You should see the agent planting the seeds. When he finishes, it should start raining.

CHALLENGE
Create another command and name it "sun" to make the weather clear again. What blocks should you use?

Use a loop to repeat the agent's action twice in the "turn" function.

TROUBLESHOOTING
If you think that the player moves far away from the agent at the end of the program, try changing the parameters in the teleport to block in the "farm" command.

Did you know?
Colonial farmers in North America (1610-1775) grew a wide variety of crops depending on where they lived. Popular crops included wheat, corn, barley, oats, tobacco, and rice.

GLOSSARY

Agent

An agent is mobile (a mob). The agent helps players learn coding by getting players to code the actions on the agent.

Colonial

Relating to or characteristic of a colony or colonies

Colony

A group of people of one nationality or race living in a foreign place

Developing world

A poor agricultural country that is trying to grow and develop socially and economically

Farming

The activity of growing crops and raising livestock

Function

A set of instructions that can be used to do an action

Inventory

The pop-up menu that the player uses to manage items they carry. From this screen, a player can equip armor, tools, and blocks, and craft items on a grid.

Loop

An instruction or set of instructions that keep repeating

Mobs

Living, moving game entities. The term "mob" is short for mobile.

Parameter

A set of numbers used to locate a point on a line, map, or grid. Usually called coordinates, they are called parameters in *Minecraft*.

Spawn

To create players and mobs and place them in the game world

Teleport

To transport a thing or person across space and distance instantly

Till

To prepare the soil by digging, stirring, and turning

FURTHER INFORMATION

BOOKS

Kids Get Coding by Heather Lyons and Elizabeth Tweedale (Lerner Publications, 2016)

WEBSITES

https://education.minecraft.net/get-started/download

INTERNET SAFETY

The internet is a great resource, which helps you connect, communicate, and be creative.

However, you need to stay safe online. Always remember:

1. If you see anything online which makes you feel uncomfortable or unhappy, tell a grown up right away.

2. Never share your personal information, such as your full name, address, or date of birth, with anybody online.

3. Remember that people online may not always be who they say they are. Never share anything with people online unless you are sure you know who they are.

Note to parents

It is advisable to:

- Use filtering software to block unwanted content

- Familiarize yourself with the privacy settings of your device

- Set up passwords to protect personal information.

INDEX